We Work Better Together

By Janice S. Lary

Based on a true story.

Welcome to our happy home!

I'm Winston and I'm a dog.

I'm Nike and I'm a cat.

getting ready to take a fun ride!

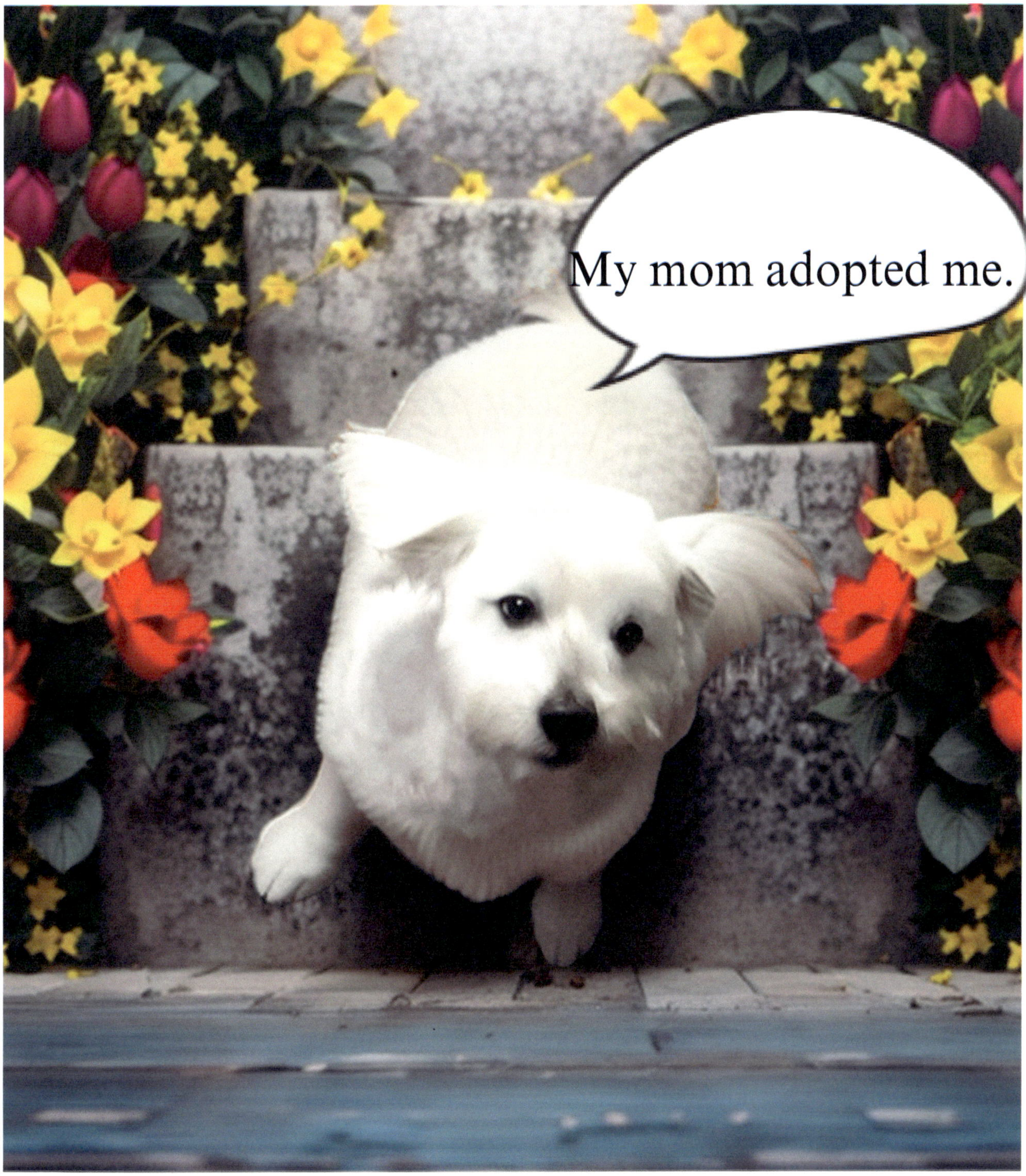
My mom adopted me.

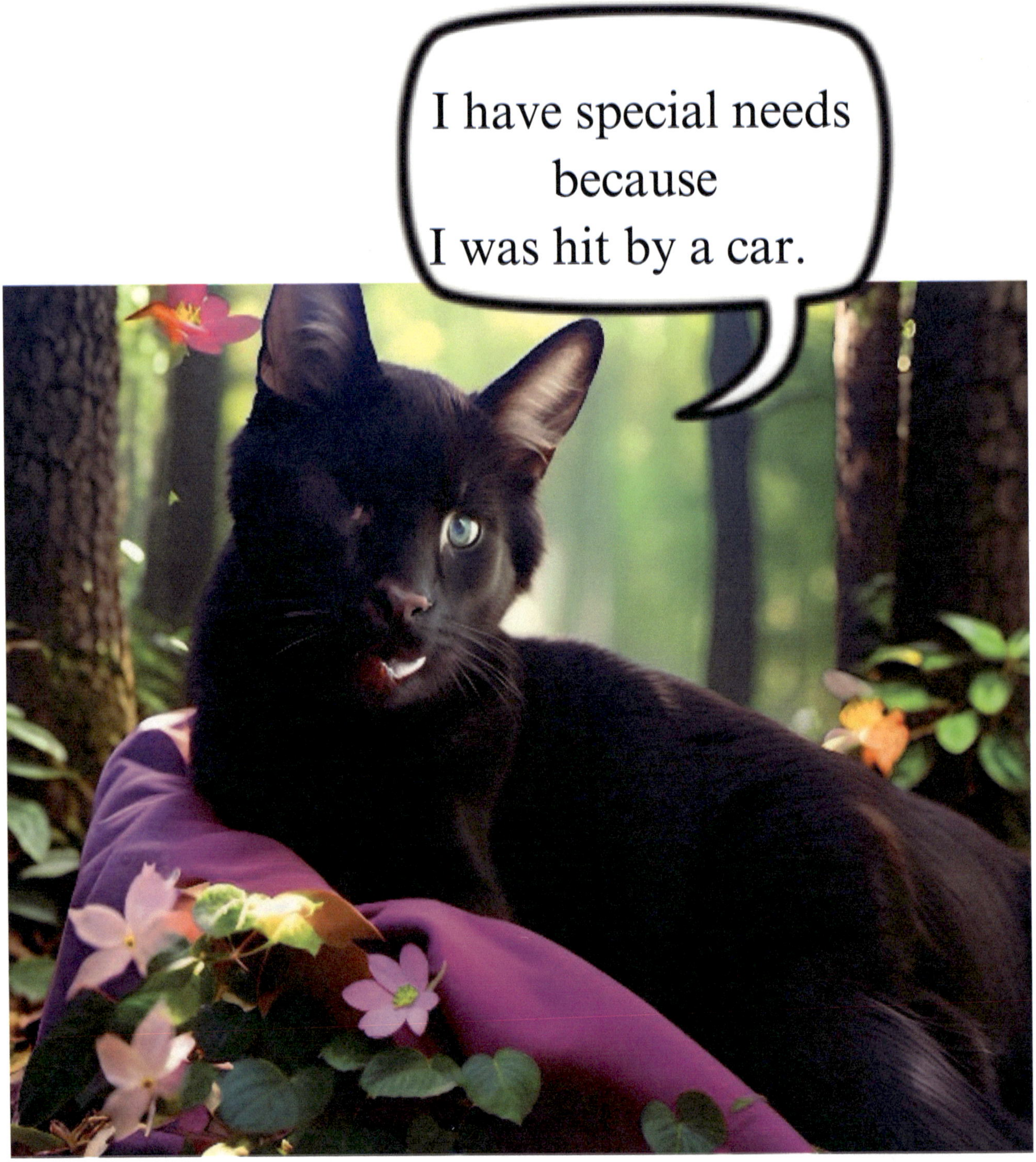
I have special needs because I was hit by a car.

I was hurt really bad! Oh no!
But I got well
and Mom brought me home

Now it's time for us to say our prayers. Now I lay me down to sleep.
I pray the Lord my soul to keep.
His love be with me through the night.
And wake me with the morning light.
And if I die before I wake.
I pray the Lord my soul to take.
In Jesus' Name.
Amen.

I love to pray.

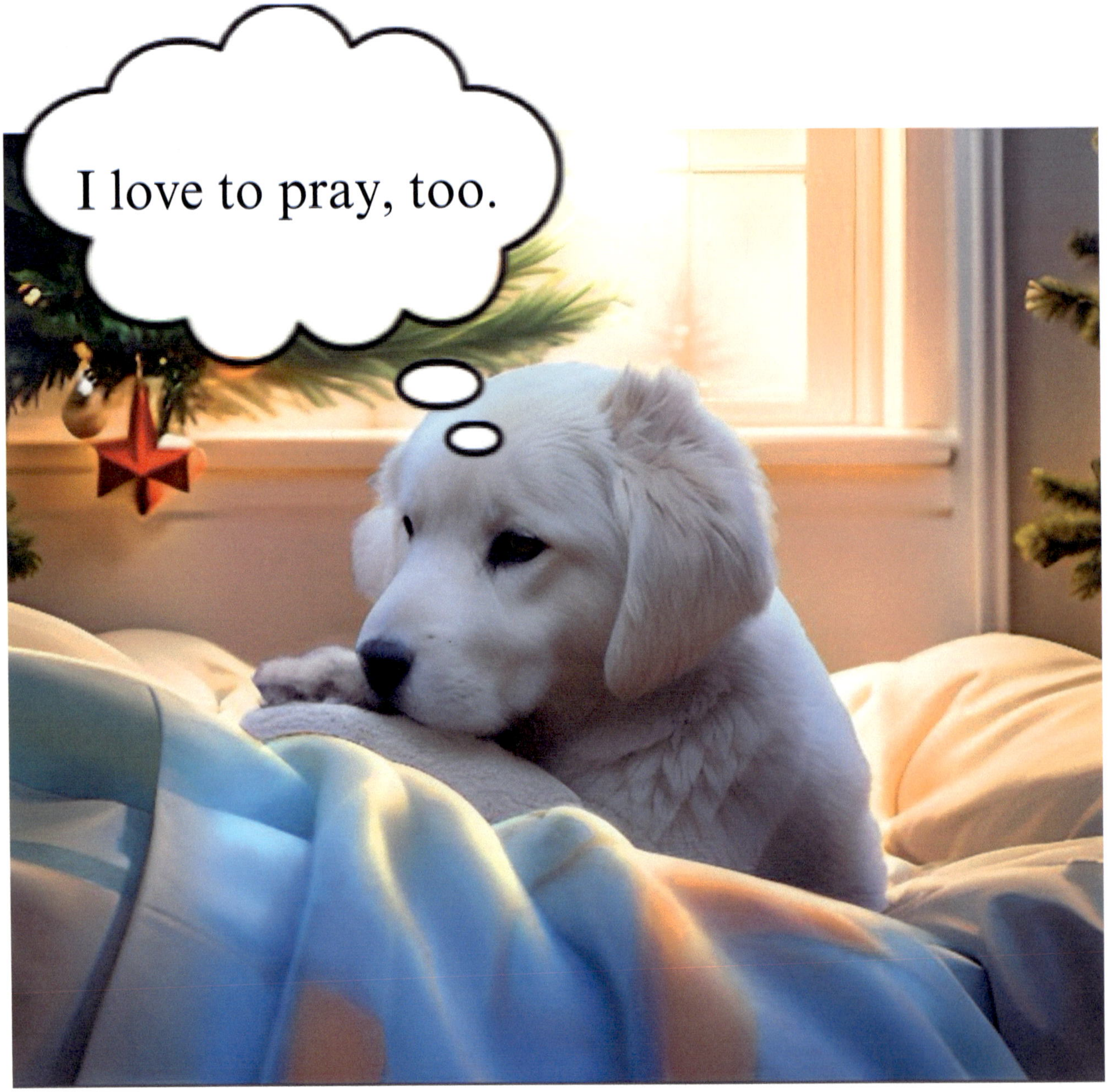
I love to pray, too.

Now it's time to take a nap together.

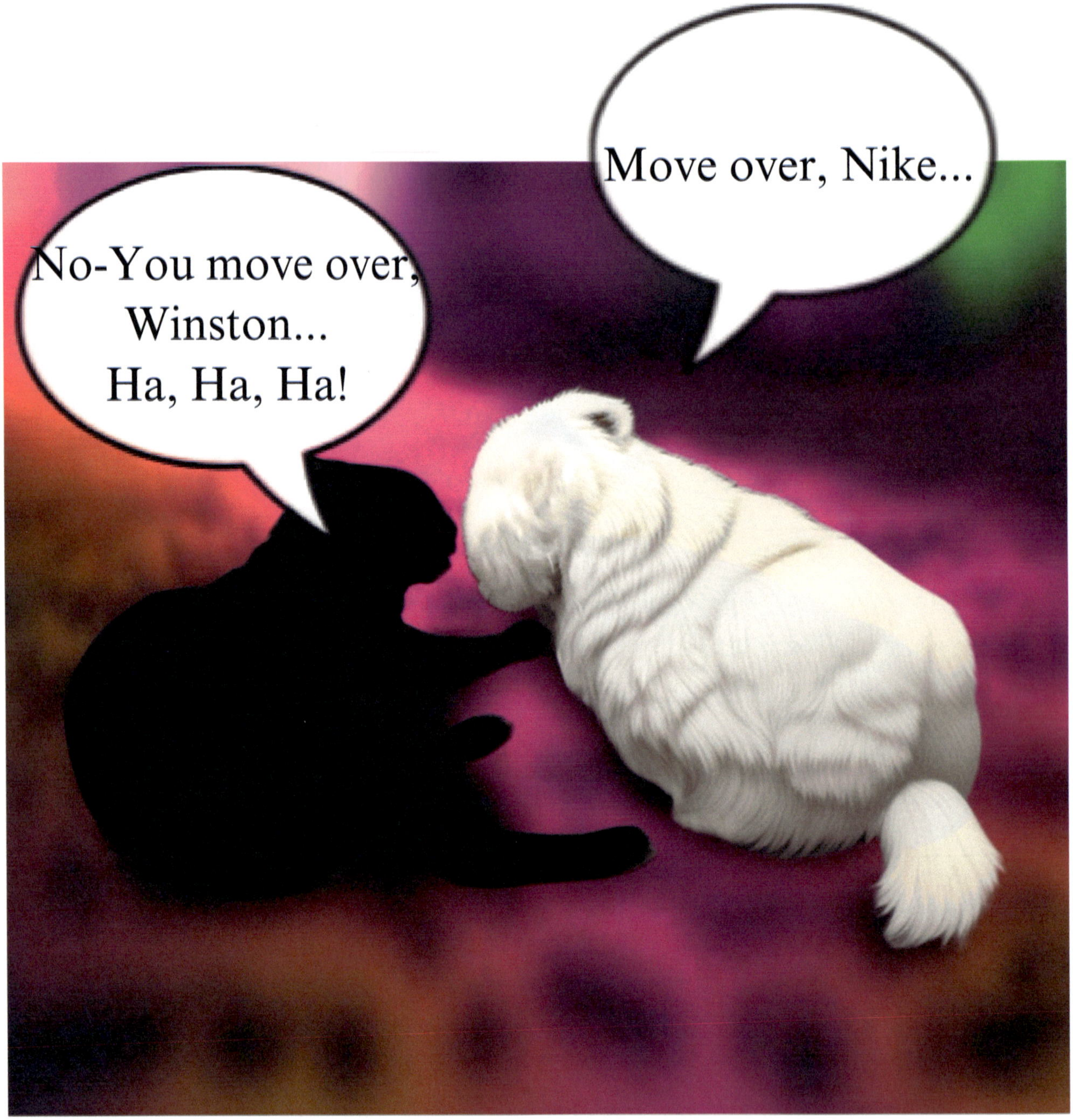
Move over, Nike...
No-You move over, Winston... Ha, Ha, Ha!

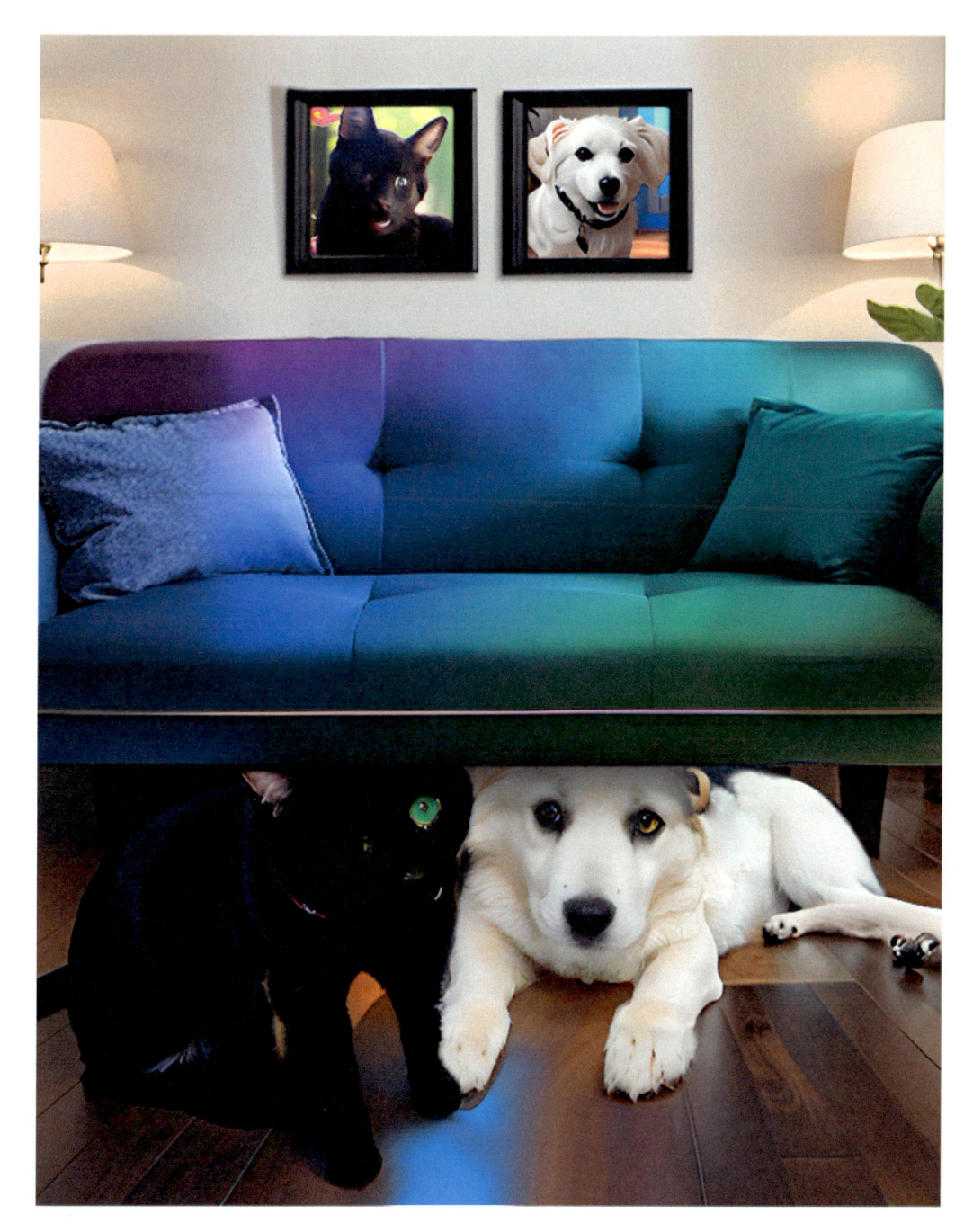

Mommy got upset one day because Winston had a "boo boo" on the floor. So, we ran under the sofa. "Okay, Mommy! We're sorry!"

"Mom said that it was okay. She told us that everyone makes mistakes."

"Now, it's bath time!"

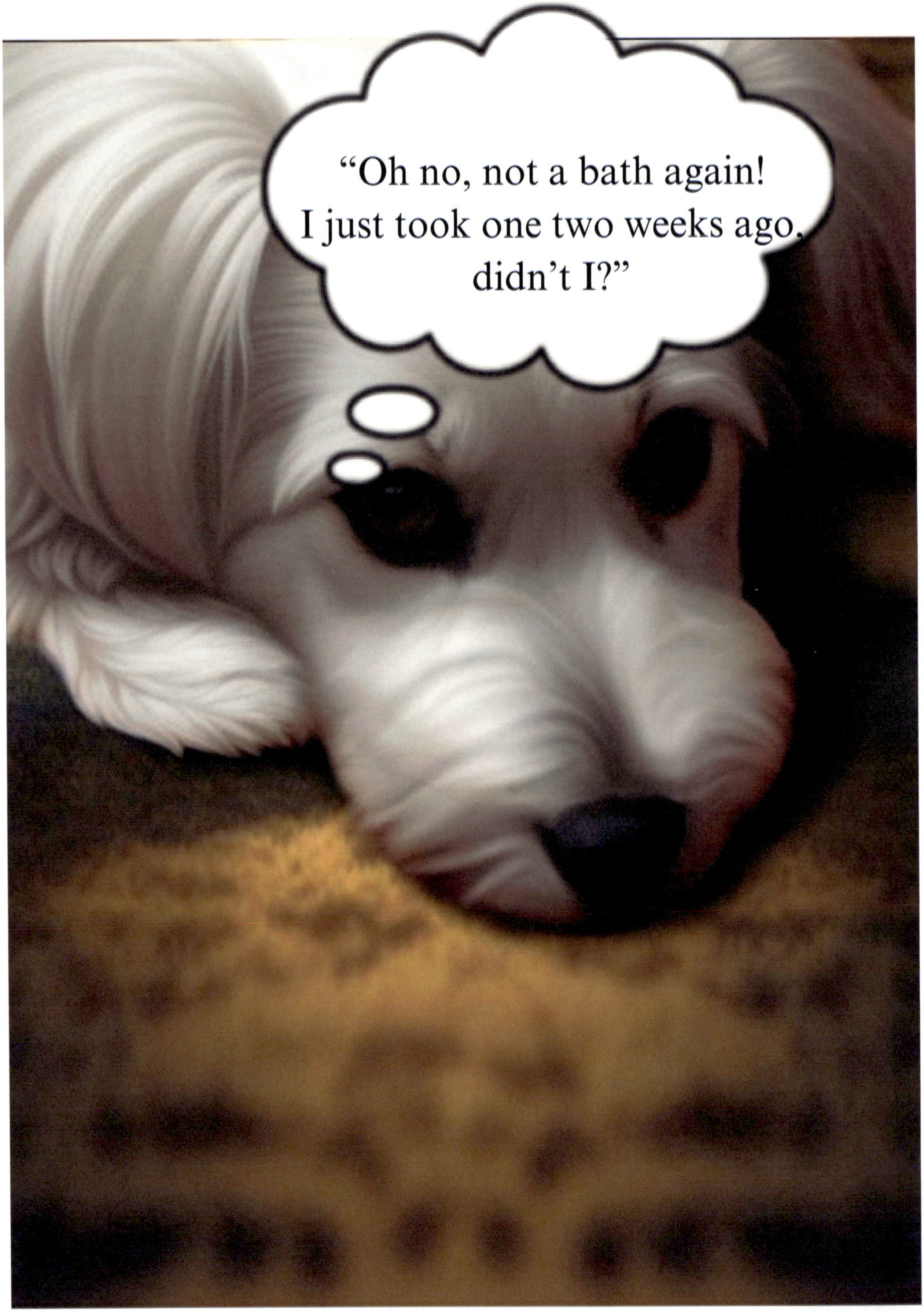
"Oh no, not a bath again! I just took one two weeks ago, didn't I?"

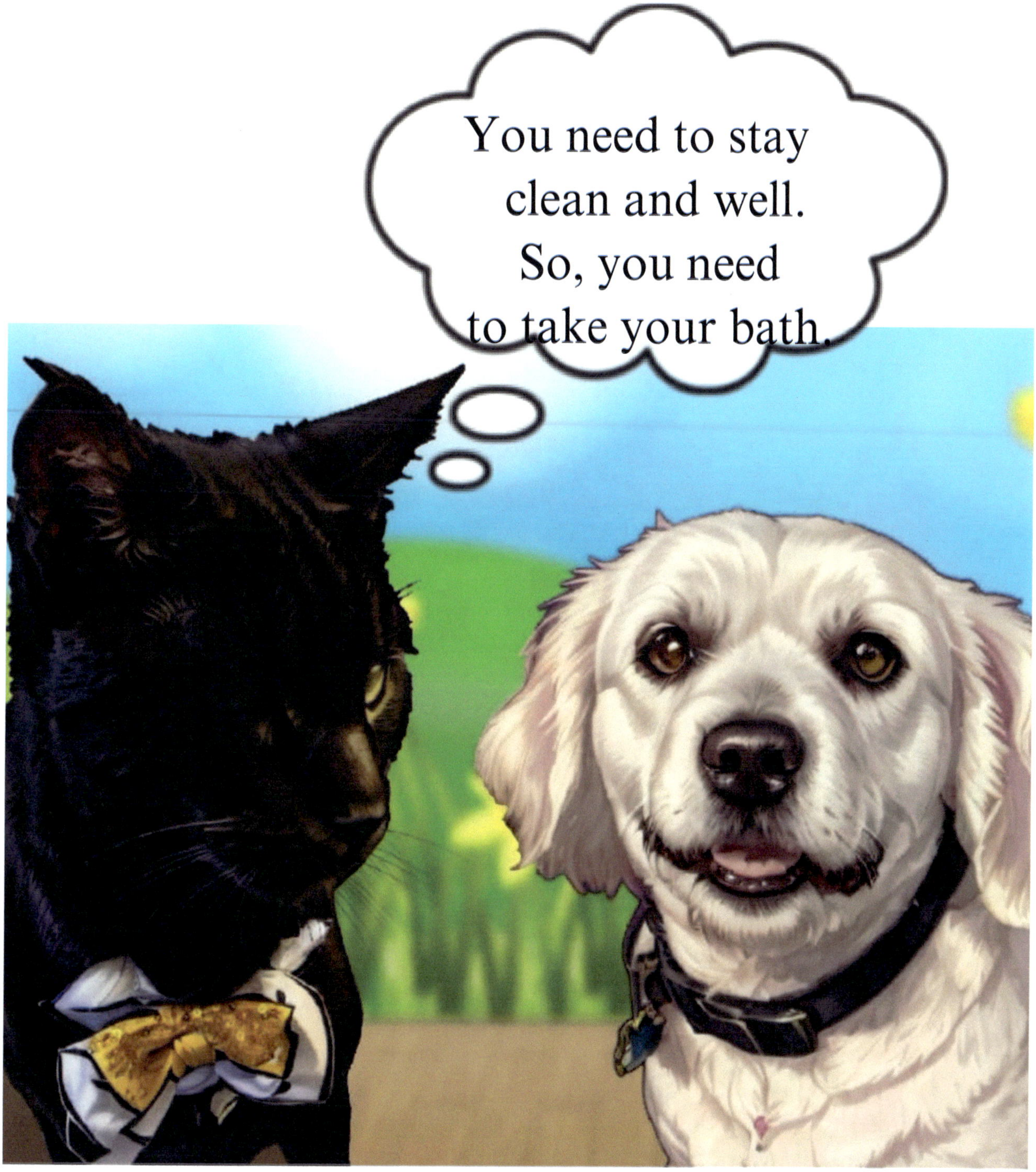
You need to stay clean and well. So, you need to take your bath.

Ha, Ha, Ha! I take my own baths, Winston...Ha, ha, ha!

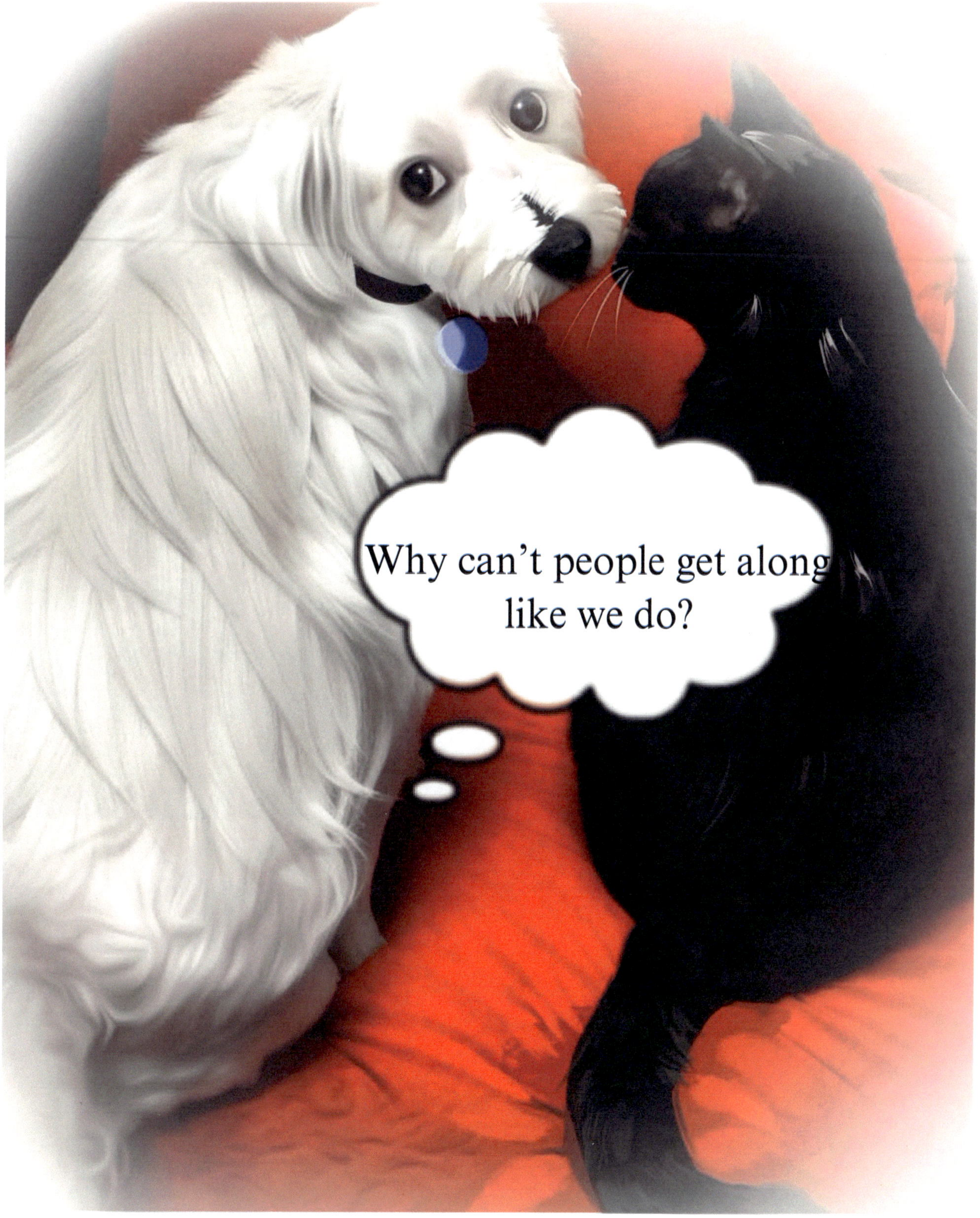
Why can't people get along
like we do?

I don’t understand it, either.
We are different.
You are a dog, and I am a cat!

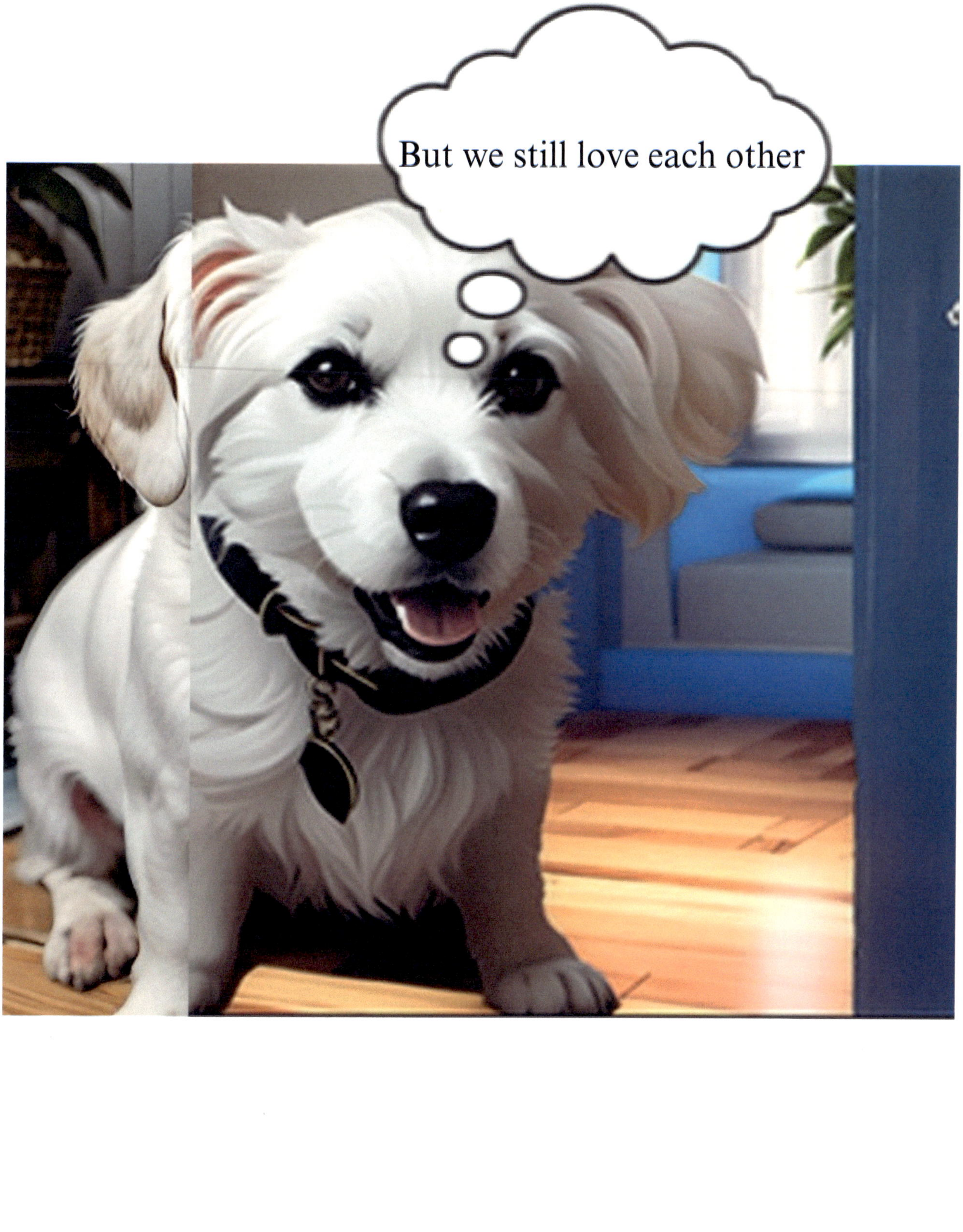
But we still love each other

Sometimes, the other cats laugh at me because I look different.

One of my teeth sticks out,Winston, and I only have one eye.
But that doesn't bother me, Nike. We are still brothers.

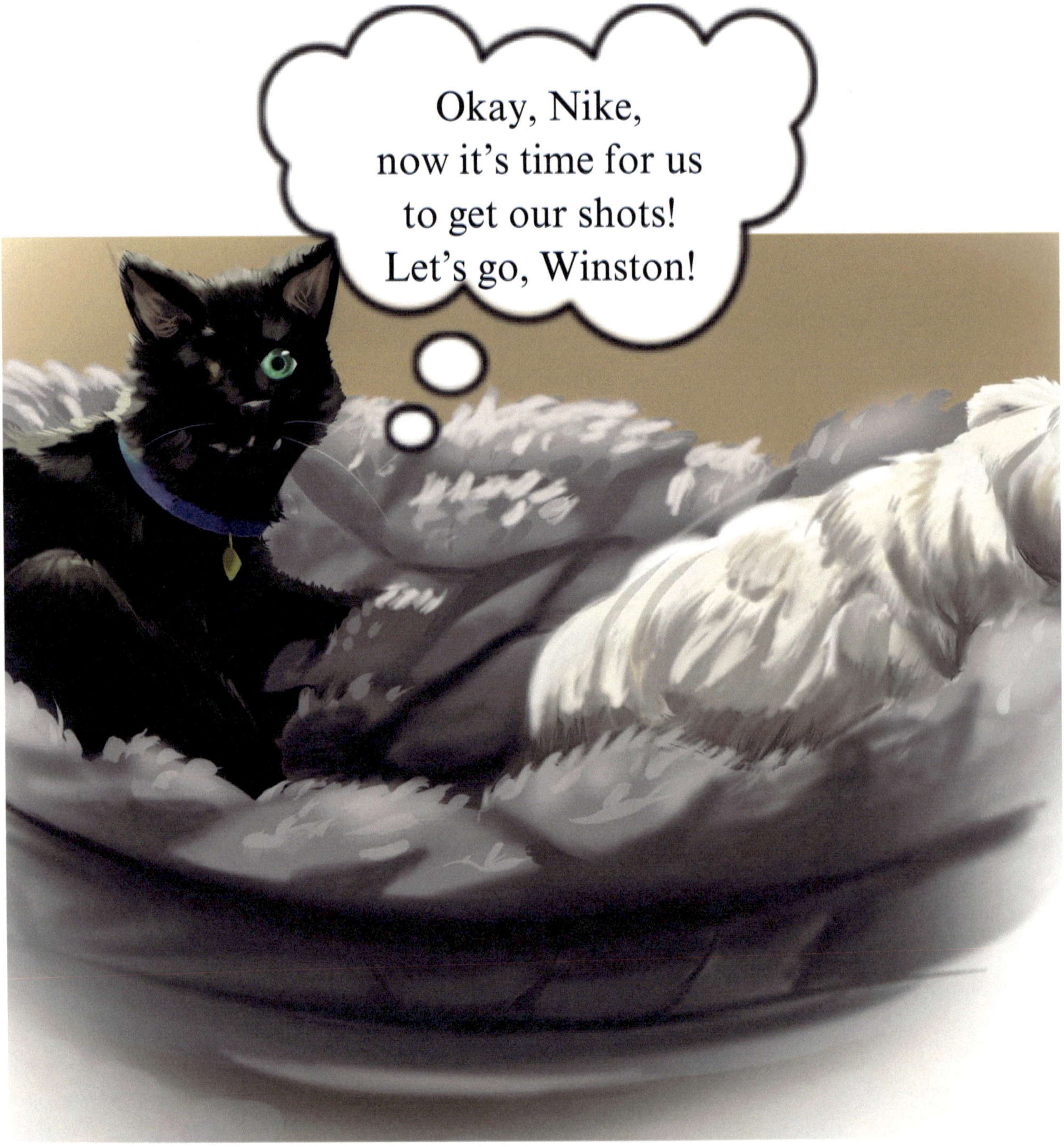
Okay, Nike,
now it's time for us
to get our shots!
Let's go, Winston!

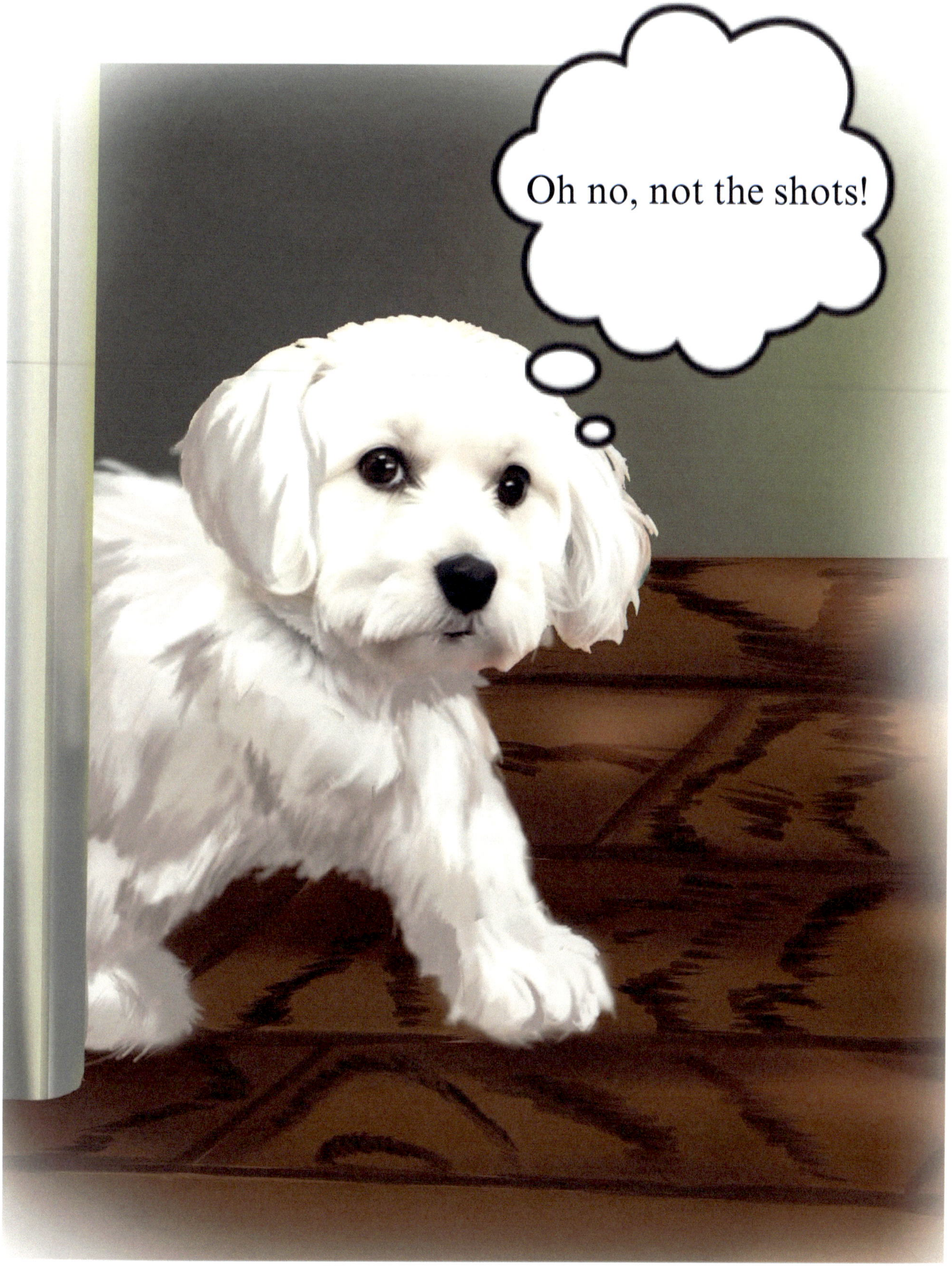
Oh no, not the shots!

That's right, Winston!
I don't like them, either!
We don't want to go!

But we need to take our shots, so we will be healthy and happy, Nike.
And it will make Mom happy too, Winston!

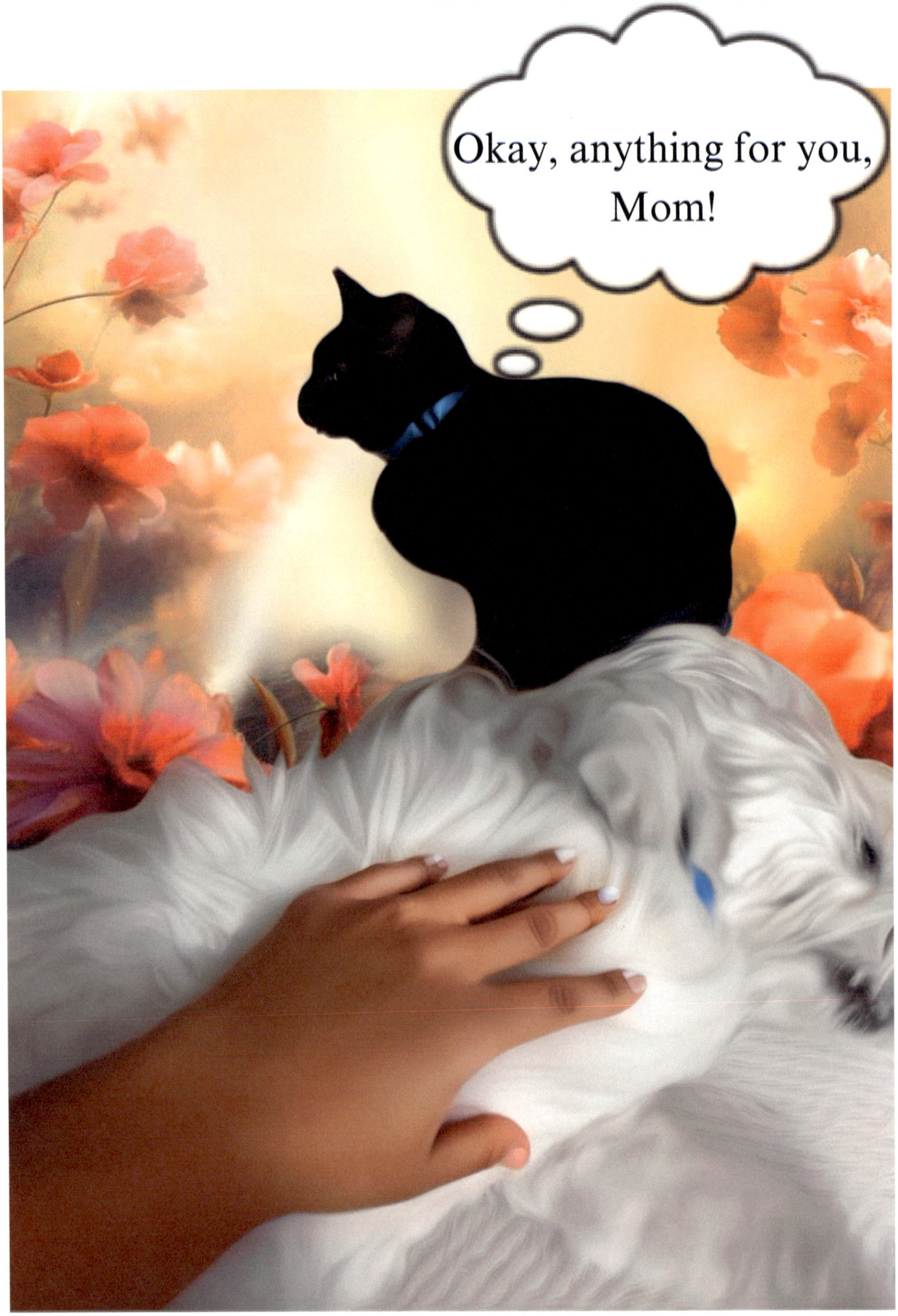
Okay, anything for you, Mom!

We have a good time.
We love each other,
even though we
may look different.

> God made each of us beautiful. And each one of us is here for a reason.

"So the family that prays together stays together."

THE END

REAL PHOTOS

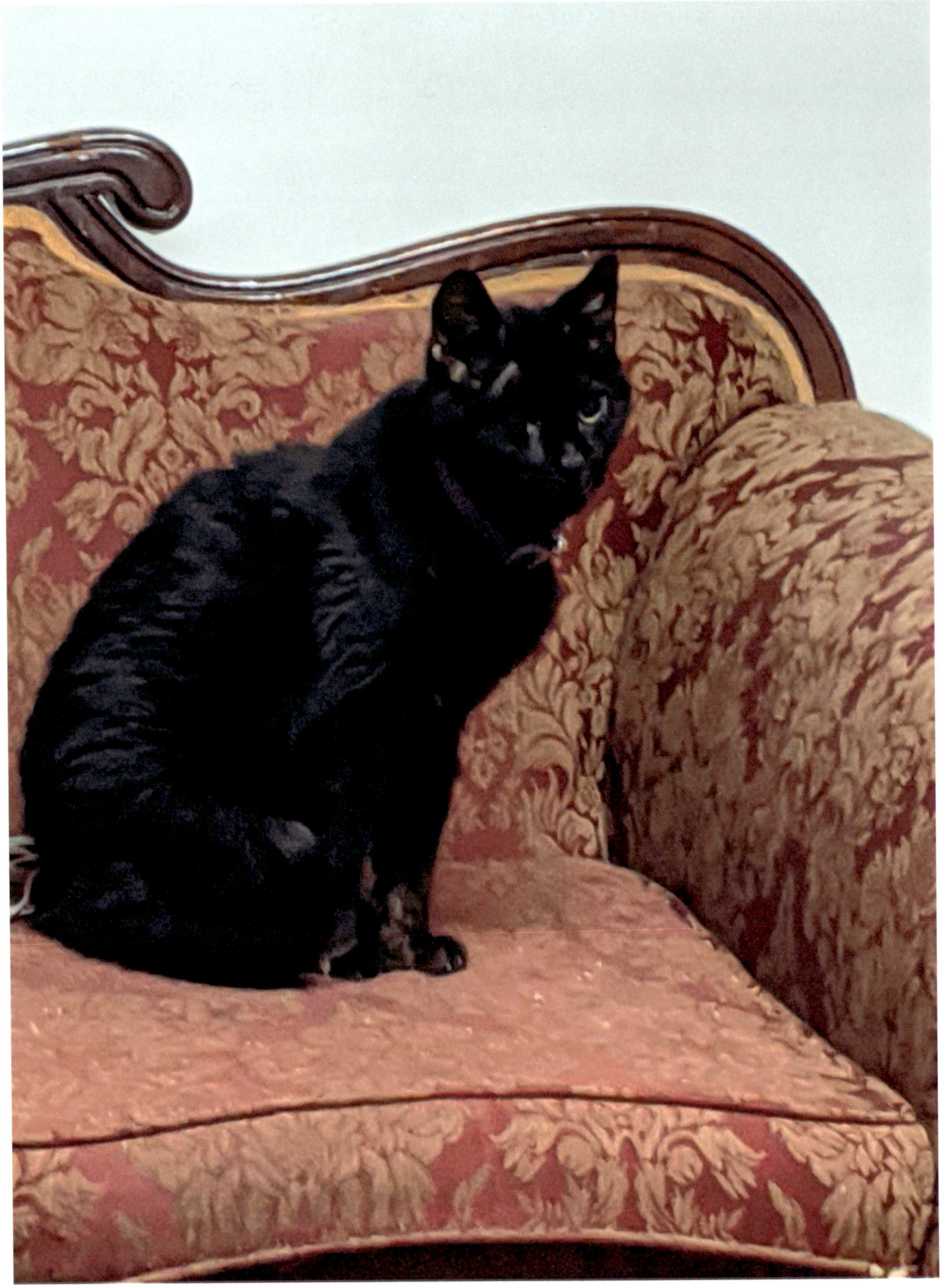

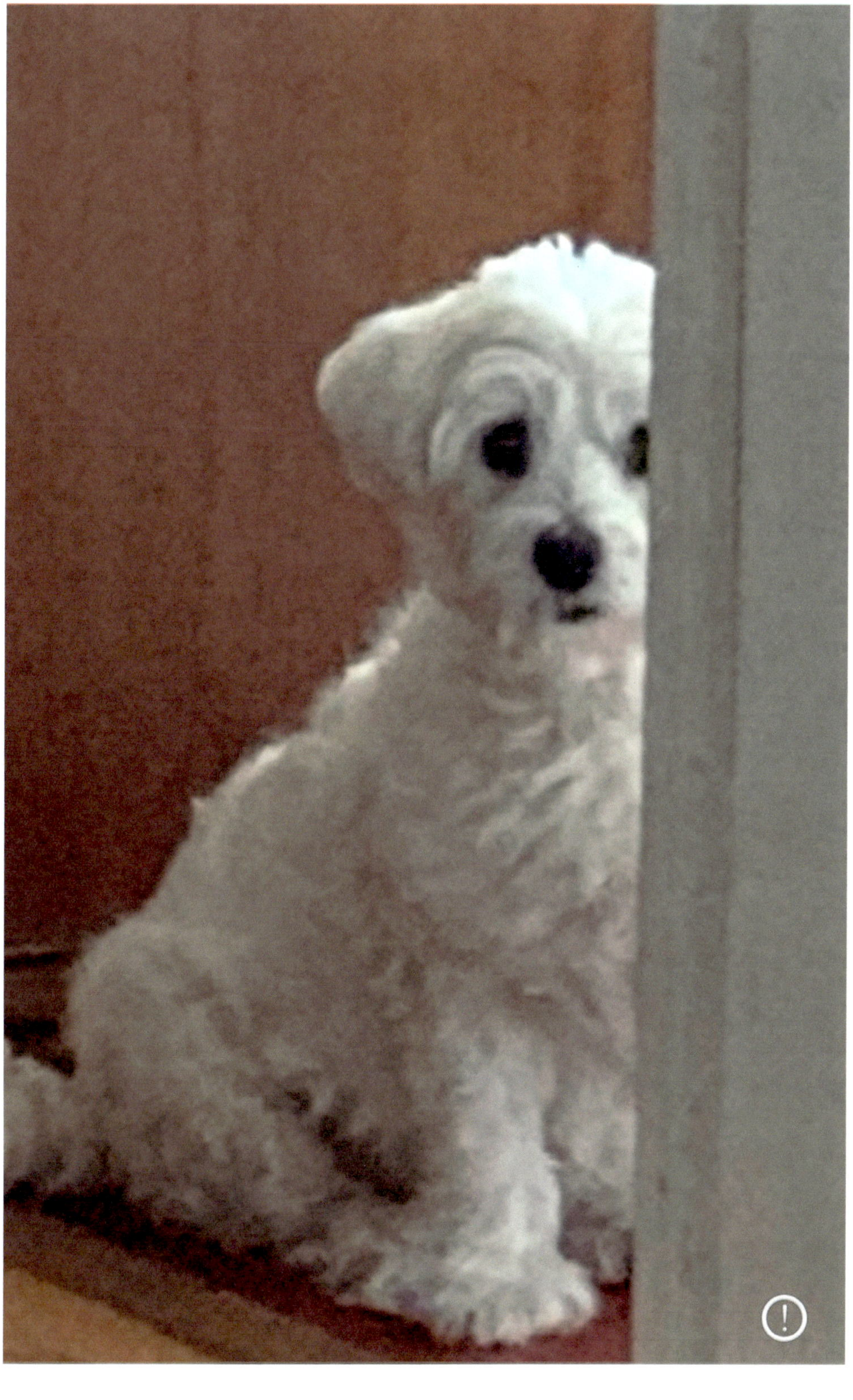

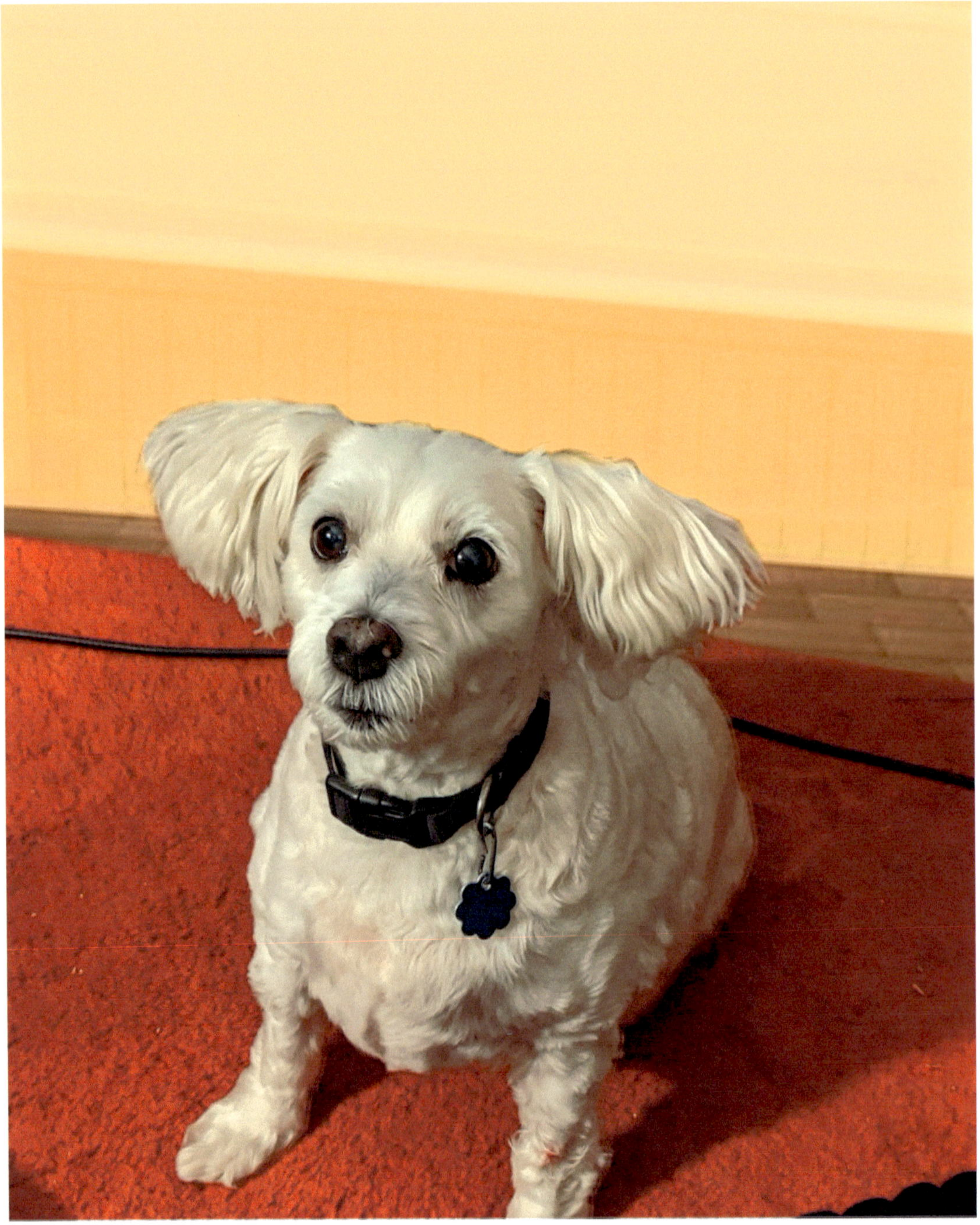

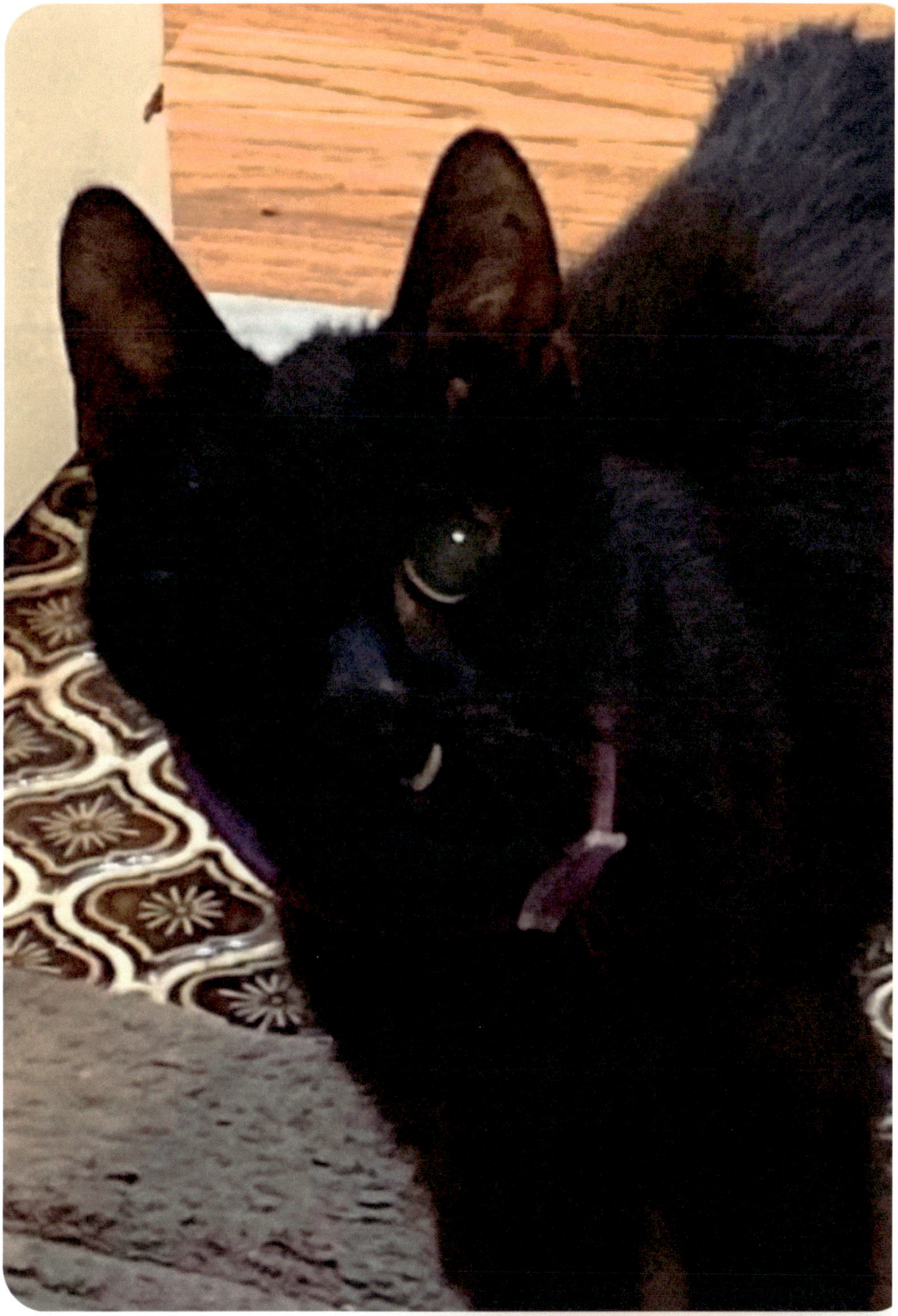

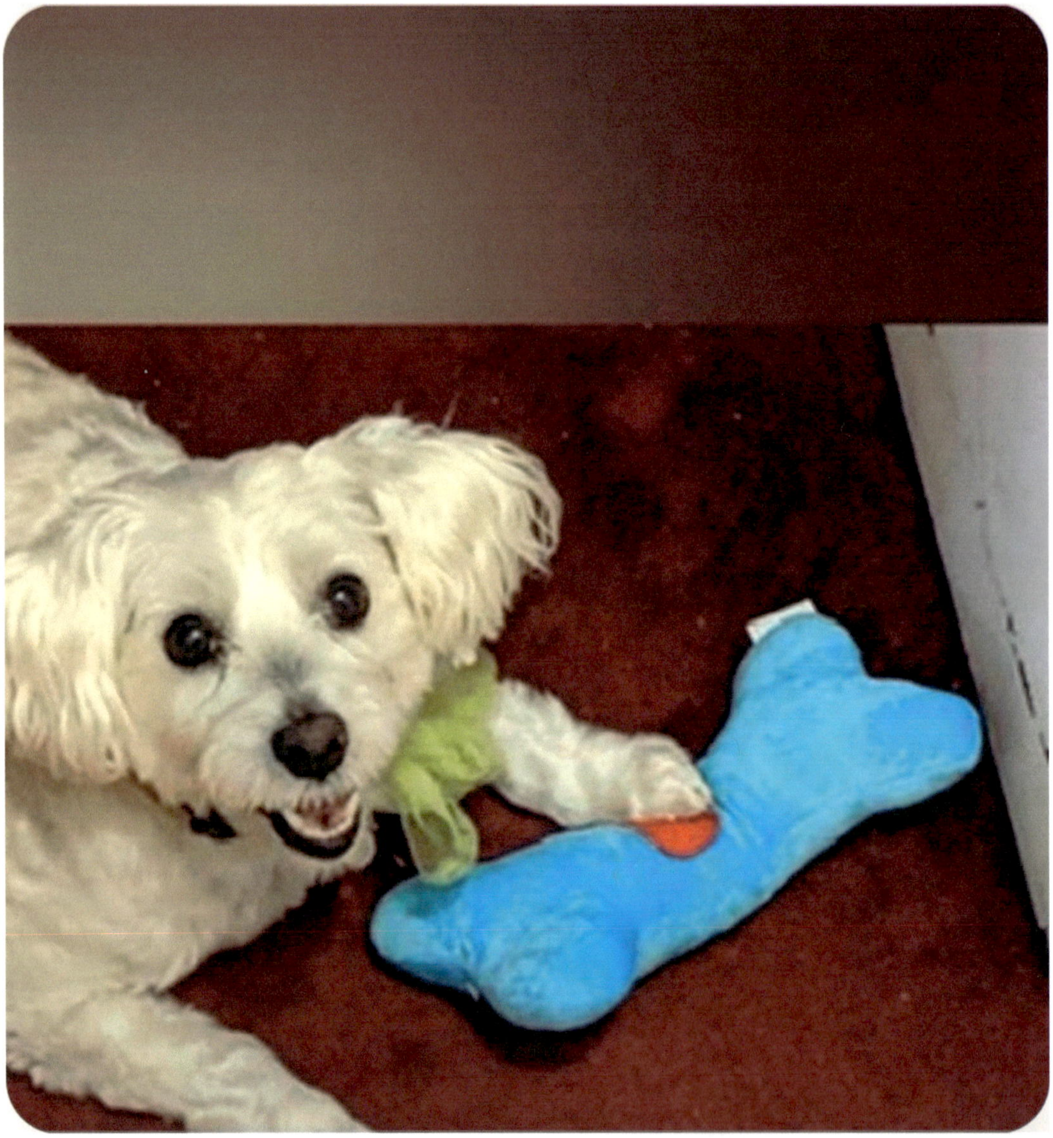

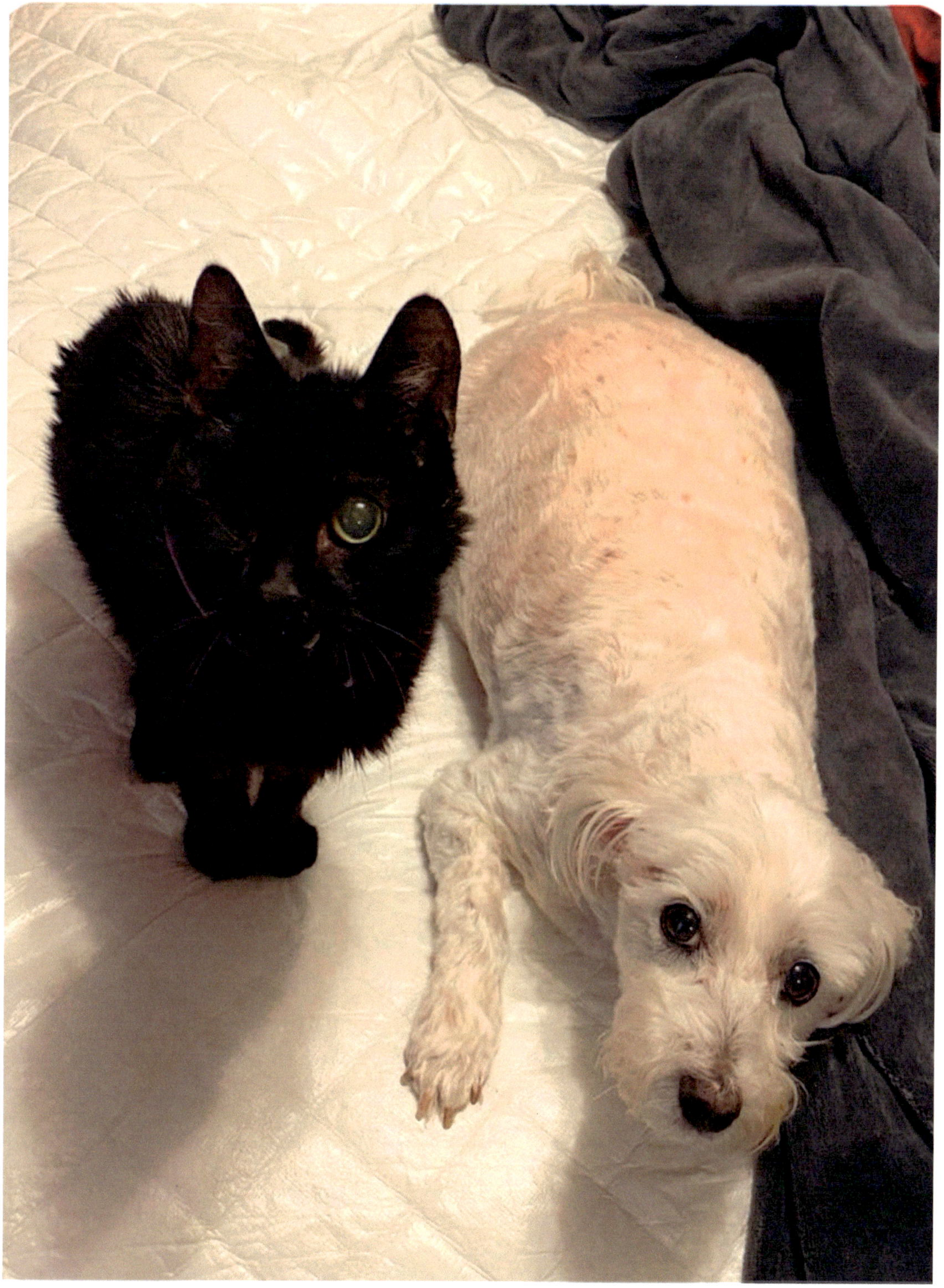

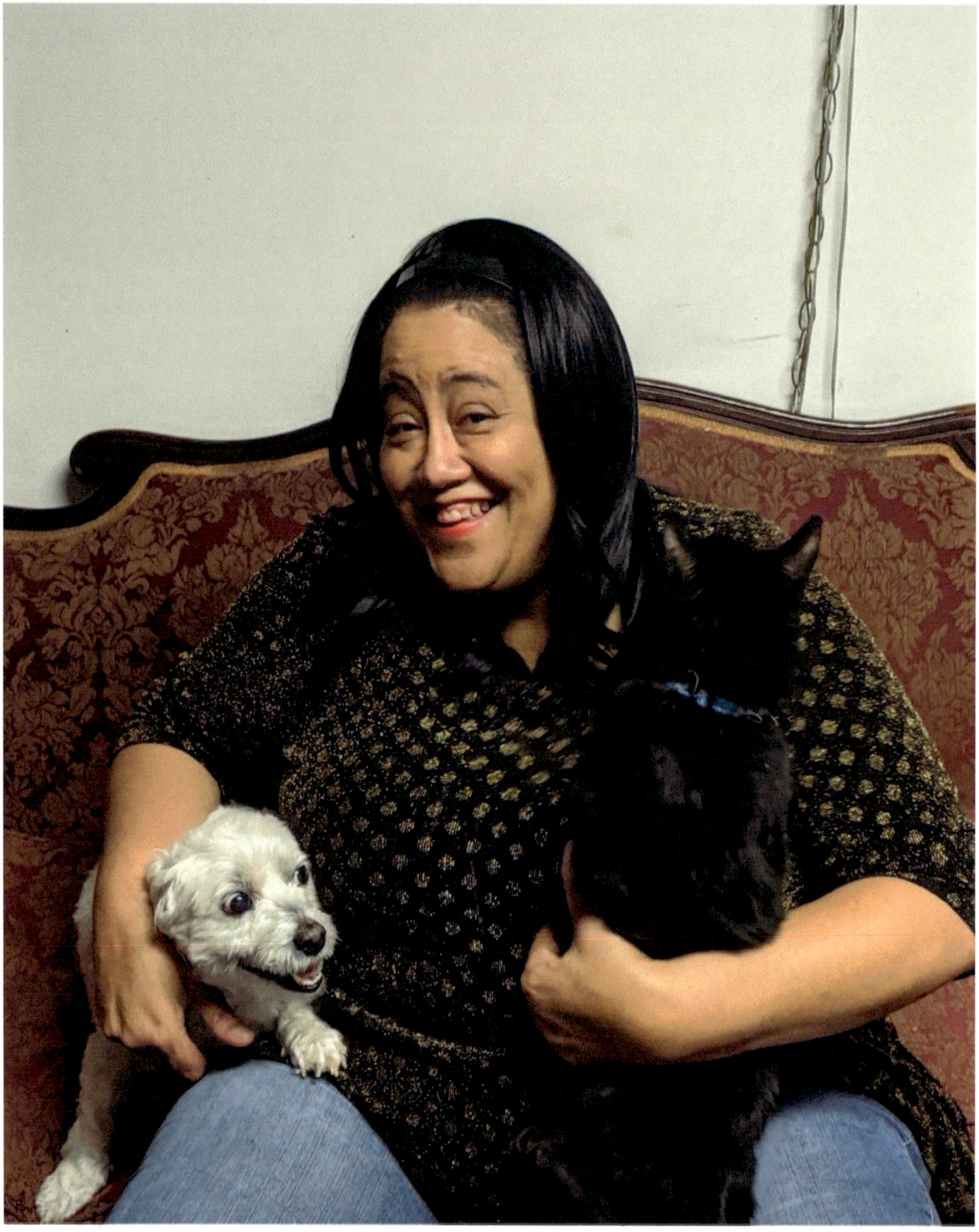

Coloring Pages

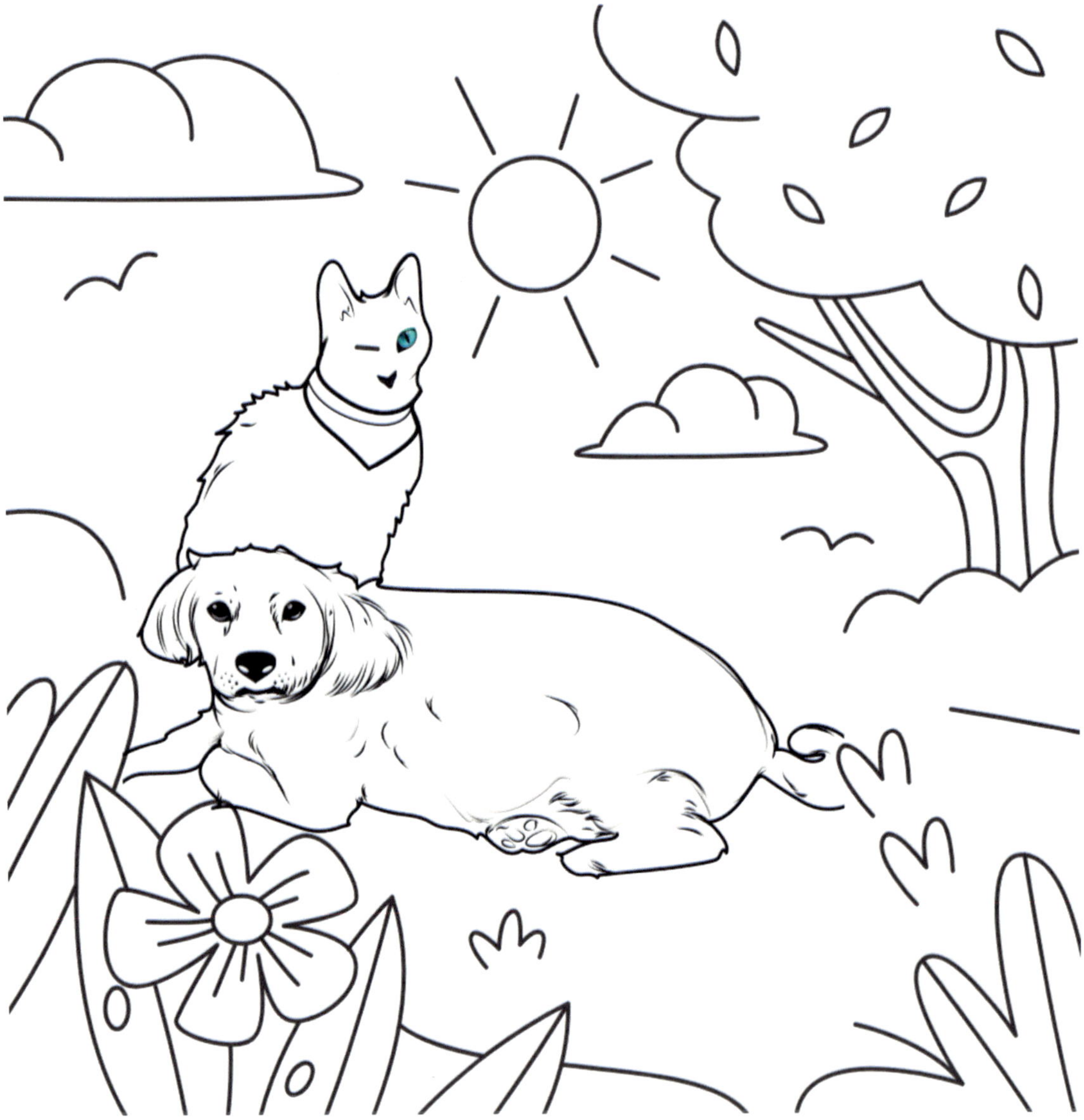

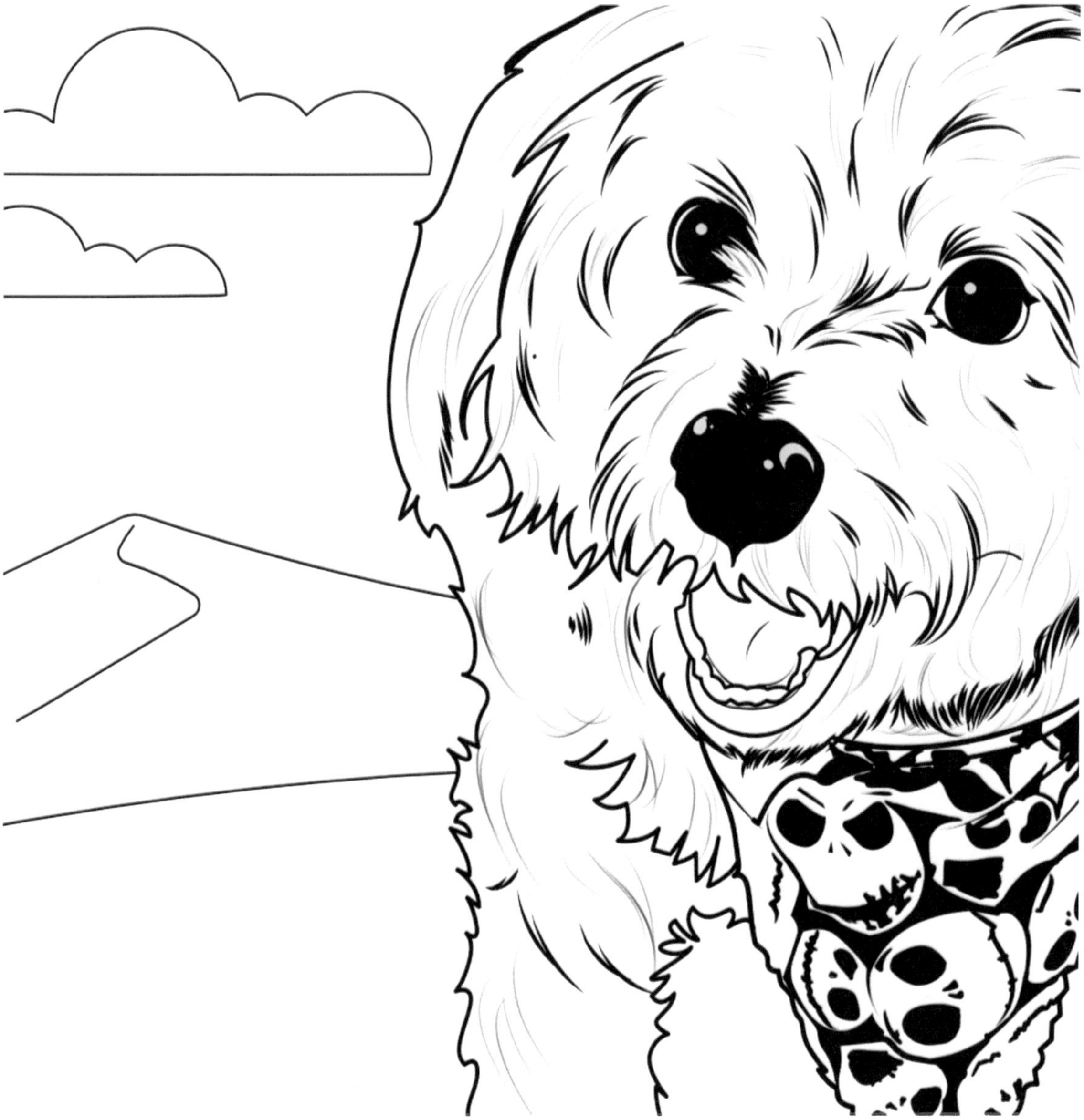

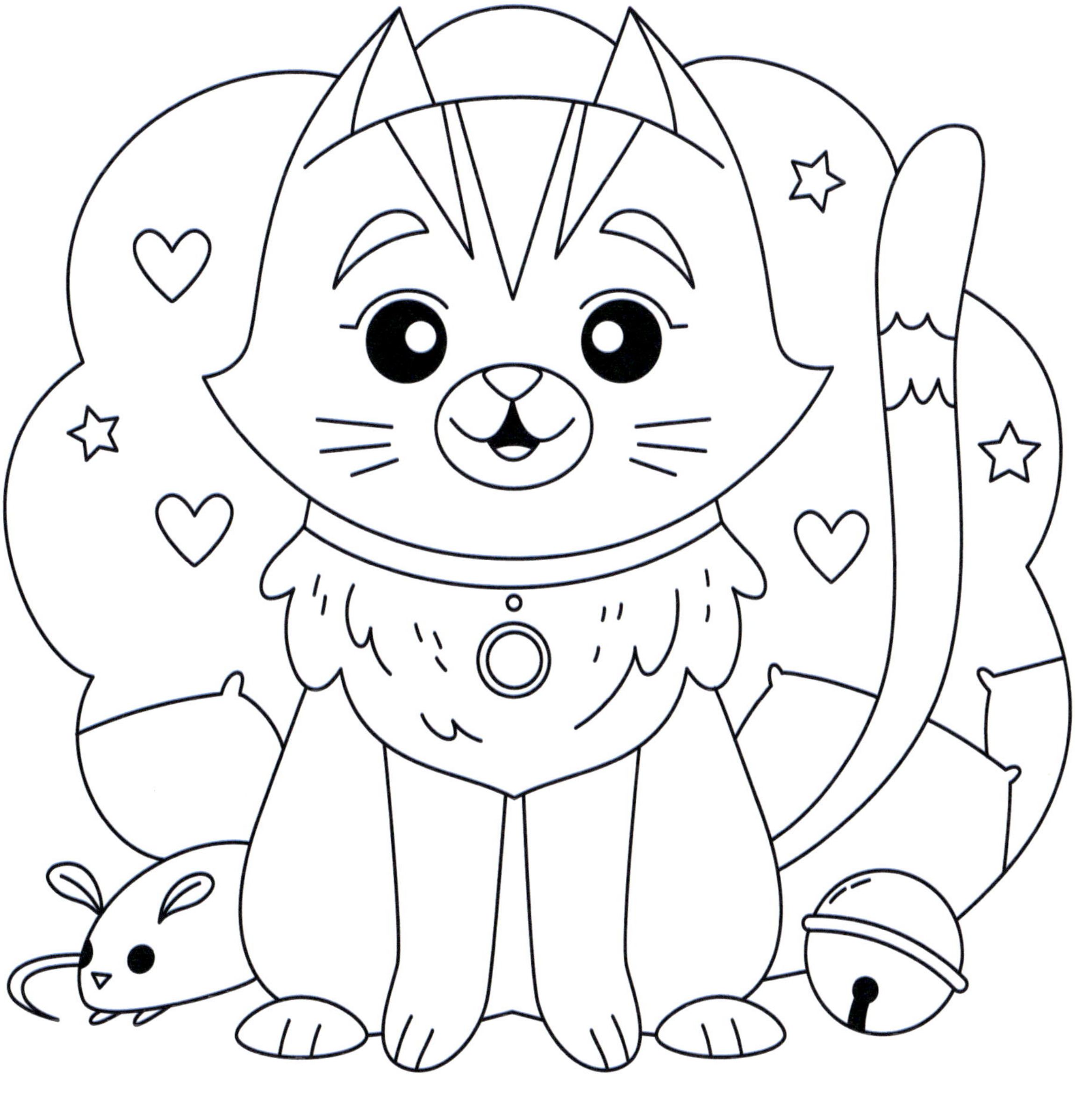

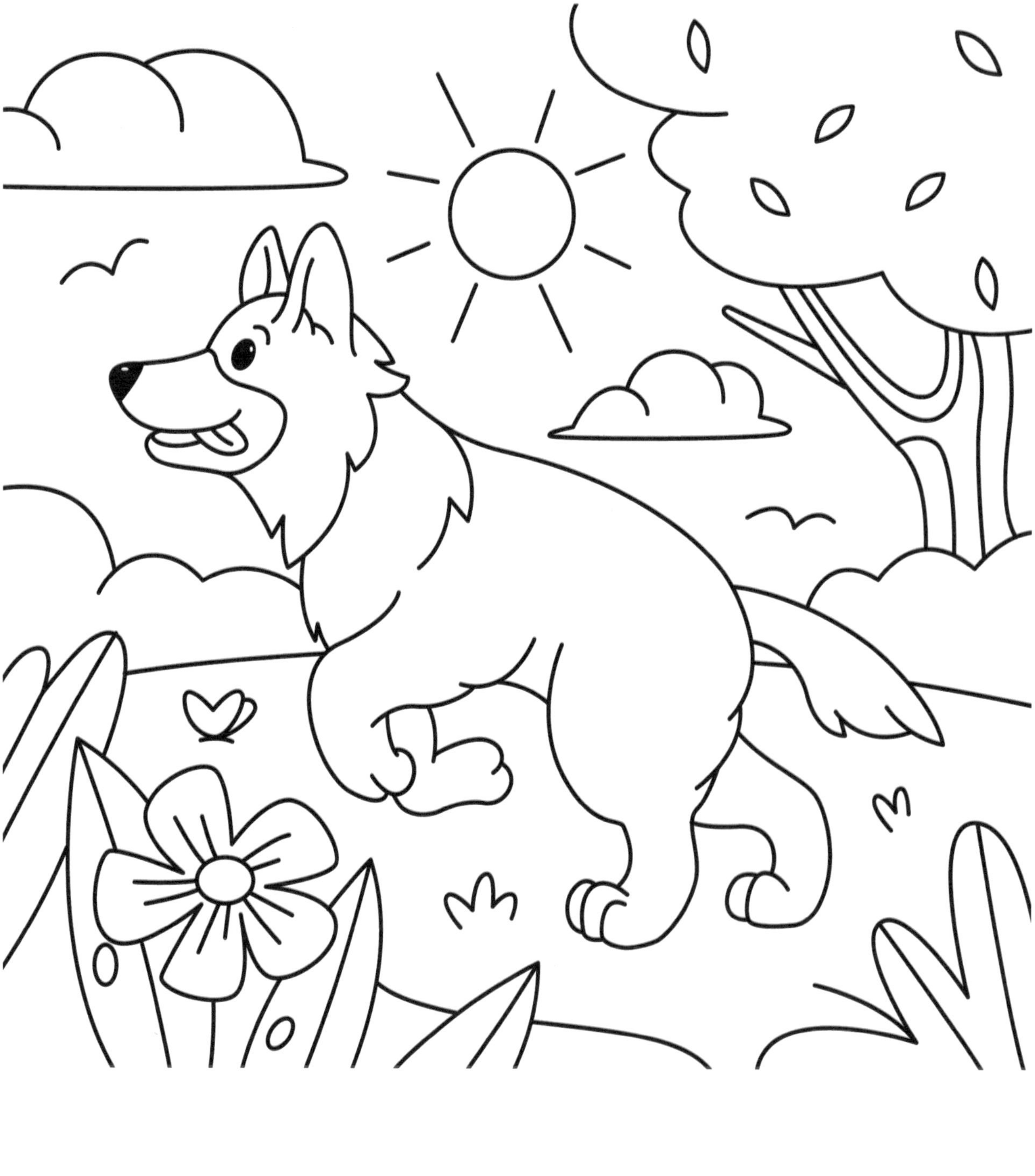

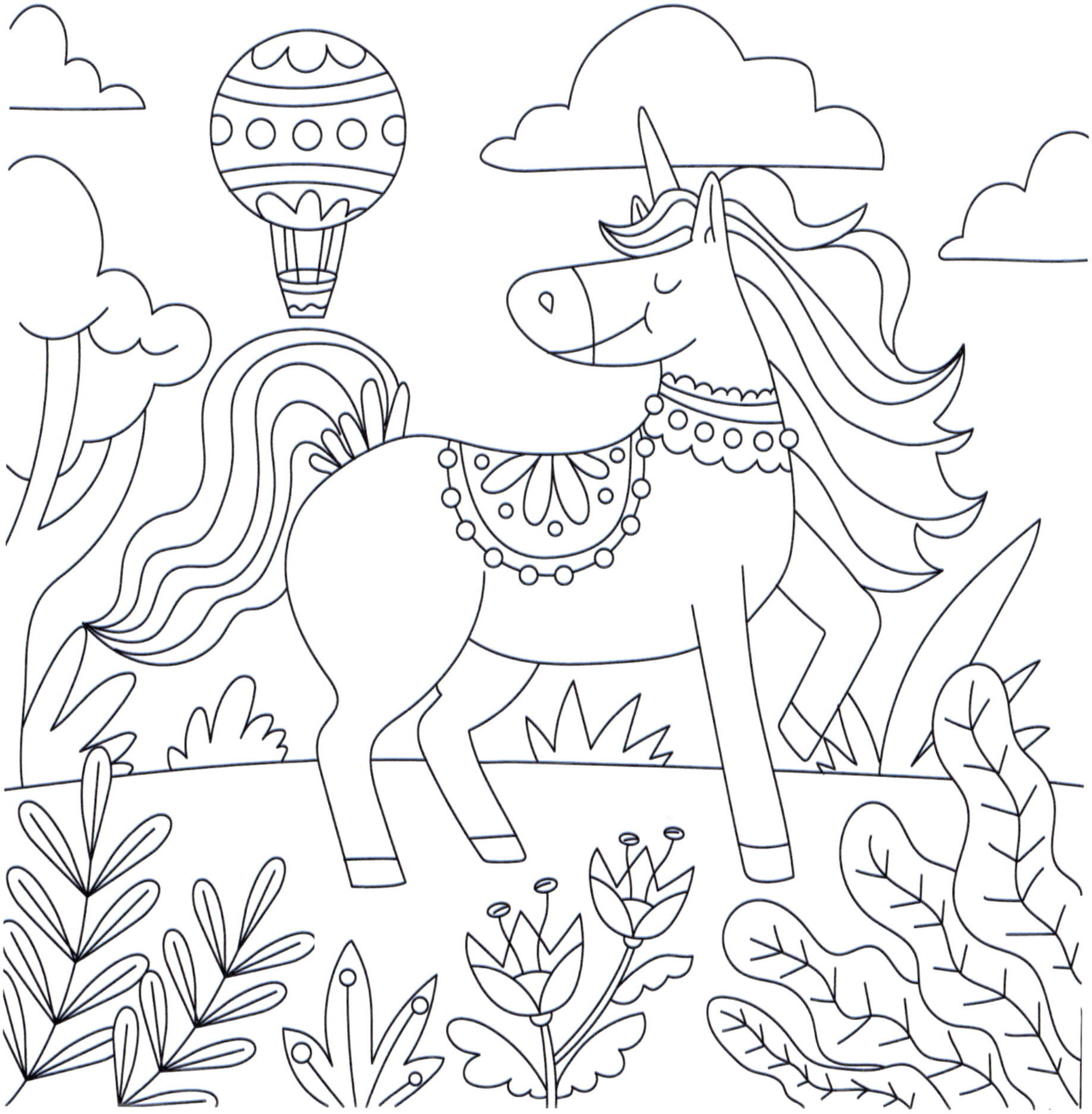

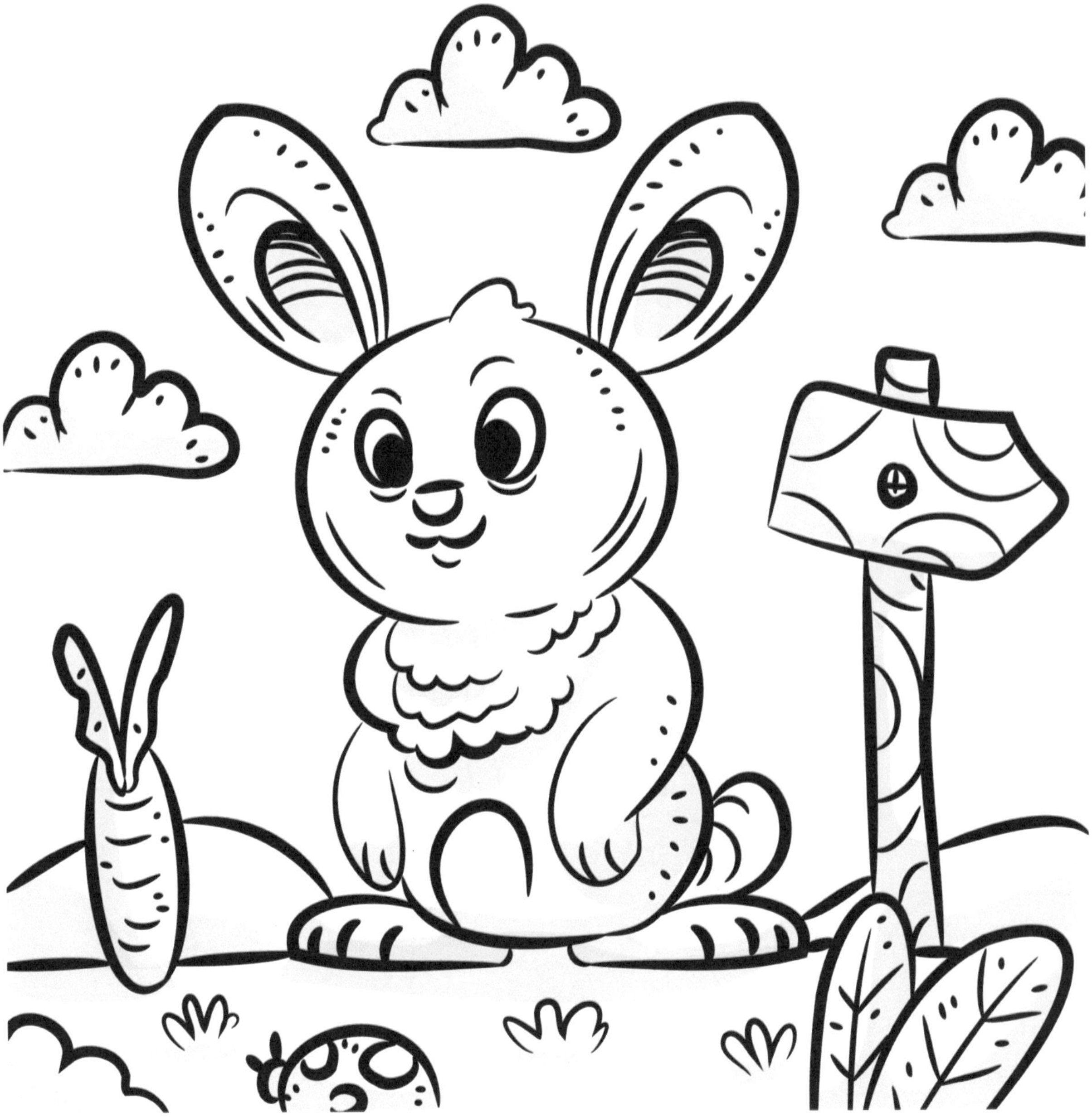

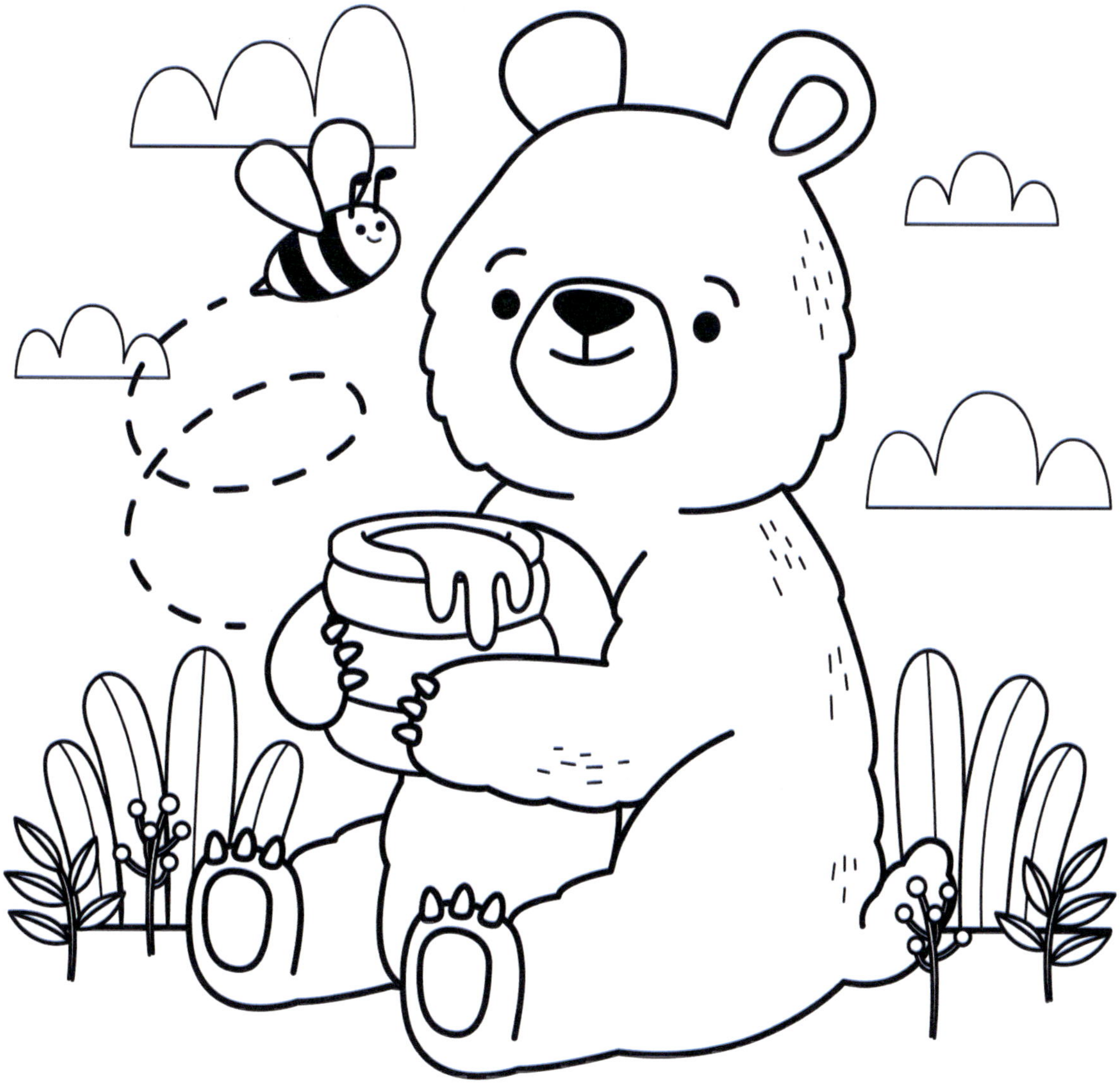

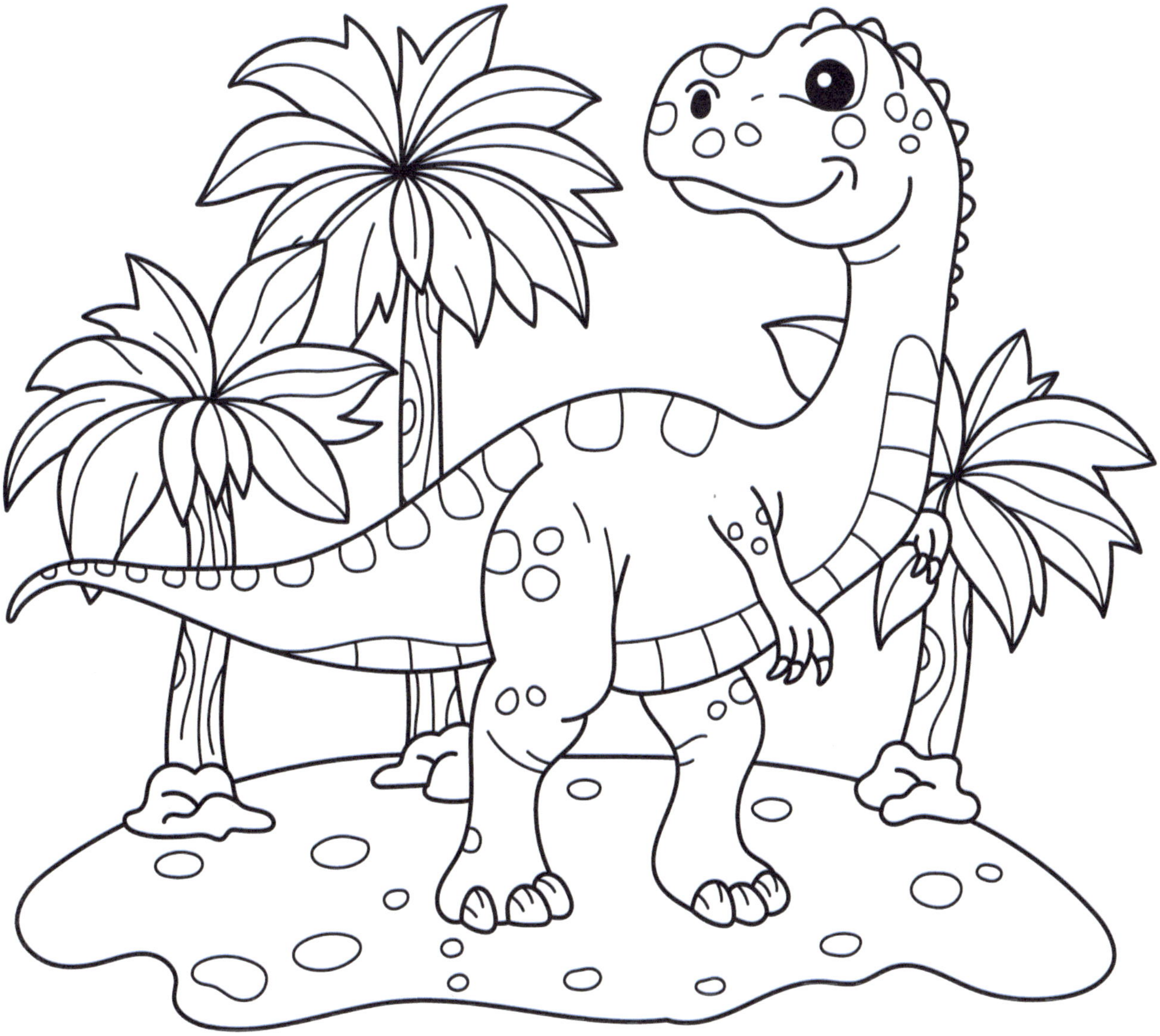

Made in the USA
Columbia, SC
10 July 2024